Exploring Careers in AI

John Allen

San Diego, CA

About the Author

John Allen is a writer who lives in Oklahoma City.

© 2025 ReferencePoint Press, Inc.
Printed in the United States

For more information, contact:
ReferencePoint Press, Inc.
PO Box 27779
San Diego, CA 92198
www.ReferencePointPress.com

ALL RIGHTS RESERVED.
No part of this work covered by the copyright hereon may be reproduced or used in any form or by any means—graphic, electronic, or mechanical, including photocopying, recording, taping, web distribution, or information storage retrieval systems—without the written permission of the publisher.

Picture Credits:
Cover: PeopleImages.com-Yuri A/Shutterstock
4: Shutterstock
6: Andrey_Popov/Shutterstock
11: dennizn/Shutterstock
14: Monkey Business Images/Shutterstock
16: panuwat phimpha/Shutterstock
20: Poetra.RH/Shutterstock
23: Fizkes/Shutterstock
25: Gorodenkoff/Shutterstock
29: wear it out/Shutterstock
32: gonzagon/Shutterstock
35: Vadym Pastukh/Shutterstock
38: Ascannio/Shutterstock
41: MDV Edwards/Shutterstock
43: Artie Medvedev/Shutterstock
47: NASA
50: Chay-Tee/Shutterstock
52: wee dezighn/Shutterstock

LIBRARY OF CONGRESS CATALOGING-IN-PUBLICATION DATA

Names: Allen, John, 1957- author.
Title: Exploring careers in AI / by John Allen.
Other titles: Exploring careers in artificial intelligence
Description: San Diego, CA : ReferencePoint Press, Inc., 2025. | Includes bibliographical references and index. | Audience term: Teenagers
Identifiers: LCCN 2024044848 (print) | LCCN 2024044849 (ebook) | ISBN 9781678210083 (library binding) | ISBN 9781678210090 (ebook)
Subjects: LCSH: Artificial intelligence--Vocational guidance--Juvenile literature. | Computer science--Vocational guidance--Juvenile literature.
Classification: LCC QA76.25 .A44 2025 (print) | LCC QA76.25 (ebook) | DDC 006.3023--dc23/eng/20240925
LC record available at https://lccn.loc.gov/2024044848
LC ebook record available at https://lccn.loc.gov/2024044849

CONTENTS

AI Careers at a Glance	4
Introduction An Explosion of New Jobs in AI	5
Chapter One How AI Is Reshaping the Workplace and the World	9
Chapter Two Jobs and Careers in AI	18
Chapter Three Preparing for a Career in AI	27
Chapter Four Challenges of Working with AI	36
Chapter Five A Bright Future for a New Technology	45
Source Notes	54
Interview with a Software Developer	57
Find Out More	60
Index	62

AI CAREERS AT A GLANCE

AI-Related Job Postings
As of February 2024, 2% of total US jobs posted

Highest-Paying Jobs in AI*
- AI Engineer: $160,757
- Computer Vision Engineer: $168,803
- Business Development Manager: $196,491

Average Salary
Entry-Level Generative AI Engineer: $80,000

AI Skills Training

Can boost salaries by up to 30%

Required Degree
Typically, at least a bachelor's degree in computer science or mathematics

Projected Growth for AI careers
21% growth by 2031

Essential Characteristics for AI Workers
- Communication
- Critical thinking
- Problem-solving
- Teamwork

AI in the Workplace
As of August 2024, about 266 million companies were using or planning to use AI

* Average salaries

INTRODUCTION

An Explosion of New Jobs in AI

Anna Bernstein never thought of herself as an engineer, but that is part of her job description at Copy.ai, an artificial intelligence (AI) firm in New York City. Bernstein is a prompt engineer, writing text-based prompts that teach AI apps how to create blog posts or respond to customers' questions more accurately. Her job does not require technical code-writing skills. Instead, it calls for an ability to write prose with great clarity. An English major in college, Bernstein did copywriting and historical research before landing her new job. "I had no tech background whatsoever," she says. "But to have a humanities background in this field seems to me like a triumph, especially since part of the point of developing AI is to imitate human thought."[1]

Bernstein's work as prompt engineer is part of an explosion of new jobs in AI. Experts say that Generation Z is getting a boost in its employment outlook due to its exposure to AI technologies from an early age. Using AI to accomplish everyday tasks is becoming second nature to young people today. "The students will use [generative] AI no matter what they are told," says Kevin Surace, a tech innovator and entrepreneur. "That's actually a good thing, as when they graduate, employers will expect them to be experts with all majors' accessible AI platforms. . . . Blog post? All will be generated by AI, then human-edited and posted in minutes. Ad copy? Sorry, AI wins."[2]

Automating and Innovating to Perform Workplace Tasks

Technology experts and tech-savvy investors have long predicted that artificial intelligence would be a game changer for the workplace. AI develops and uses computer systems to perform tasks that ordinarily call for human intelligence. Such tasks can be simple and repetitive, like translating text, planning delivery routes, or answering customer queries. They can also be sophisticated and complex, like testing combinations of molecules to create new lifesaving drugs. AI solutions promise large time-saving benefits as well. Doctors can employ an AI app to monitor and record patient visits and fill out forms with the necessary data. This allows a physician to devote more time to each patient's needs. Office

Workers who learn to integrate AI into their daily tasks stand to be more valuable than ever. AI can be used in the manufacturing field to check electrical or filtration systems.

workers can use AI apps to sort and file documents, summarize texts, or generate ideas for customer contacts. AI can even check pieces of writing for grammar mistakes or plagiarism.

AI already is bringing sweeping changes to the ways people work. Companies say it makes their employees more productive and leads to cost savings. A January 2024 survey of chief executive officers (CEOs) by the consulting firm PwC showed how AI is altering the business landscape. In the survey, 58 percent expected generative AI (GenAI) to improve their company's products or services, and 46 percent thought it would boost profits. Also, 69 percent believed that AI will require most of their workers to develop new skills over the next three years.

Critics worry that AI's ability to perform certain tasks faster and more efficiently than a human employee will lead to huge job losses. But according to most employment experts, although there will be changes and displacements across industries, the technology is likely to create many more new jobs. Workers who learn to integrate AI into their daily tasks stand to be more valuable than ever. The key for job seekers is to approach AI as a tool and assistant, not a competitor.

Planning for an AI-Related Career

To prepare for a career in AI, it is important to think about your own skills and interests and how they align with different AI-related jobs. If you are motivated to do experiments and research, you may be suited for work as a research scientist. If you are intrigued by ethical issues around AI, you might become an ethics officer. A passion for mathematics and data analysis could lead to a career as a data scientist. If you enjoy teaching others how to use AI more effectively, you could easily find a niche as an AI educator or trainer. Those drawn to the complex algorithms of AI could help develop them as a machine-learning engineer.

Regardless of what path you choose, it is vital to get a strong background in technical skills. Classes in math and computer science are essential. Work with programming languages is also

> "AI is here to stay and the benefits of it are very clear. Our data shows that employees stand ready to embrace it for their own gain too."[3]
>
> —Sander van 't Noordende, CEO of Randstad, a Dutch recruitment company

helpful. Online courses and so-called AI boot camps offer intensive training with various aspects of AI. (The term *boot camp* refers to the intensive training period that new military recruits undergo.) Certifications earned in these courses provide a job seeker with an immediate advantage. You might even create a portfolio of work to demonstrate your expertise with AI.

As artificial intelligence continues to grow in its reach and complexity, a prospective worker in AI must keep up with new developments. It helps to consult AI-related websites and interact with others who work with the technology. Successful work in AI-related fields should be considered a lifelong commitment. "AI is here to stay and the benefits of it are very clear," says Sander van 't Noordende, CEO of Randstad, a Dutch company that specializes in finding tech workers. "Our data shows that employees stand ready to embrace it for their own gain too."[3]

CHAPTER ONE

How AI Is Reshaping the Workplace and the World

Locating the ideal candidate for a specific job can sometimes seem like a matter of luck. But Indeed, a job-finding site, is using an AI-based tool to streamline the job-search process and make it more efficient. The tool, called SmartSourcing, helps job seekers find opportunities by employing a variety of AI features. Each user uploads a résumé or fills out a profile, from which the app plucks the most relevant facts. These include education, work skills, experience, and special areas of expertise. Candidates are instantly ranked according to how well their qualifications align with job requirements. "We know that sending an application to hundreds of jobs or sending messages to hundreds of mismatched candidates only prolongs the process of actually finding a job," says Raj Mukherjee, executive vice president and general manager at Indeed. Mukherjee refers to this outdated method as "spray and pray." As he notes, "Employers don't want to sift through hundreds or thousands of résumés, and we want to make sure that we help them find the best qualified candidates to fill their role—not just the most applicants."[4] Fine-tuning the process, he says, saves employers more than eight hours per week on average.

Reshaping the Workplace with AI

Indeed's SmartSourcing is an example of how artificial intelligence is reshaping the workplace to make it more efficient. The company uses other AI apps to enhance users' job searches. One tool suggests key words and phrases to help applicants describe their work history and past achievements. Another creates a summary of a job seeker's skills and experience, giving recruiters a handy snapshot to consider. Chatbots and virtual assistants use generative AI to answer applicants' queries and help them navigate the job-search process with confidence. And Indeed is not alone in its embrace of AI solutions. Employment sites such as LinkedIn, Hired, and Phenom offer their own arrays of AI-based job-search tools, with more being added every week.

From home to work and back again, nearly everyone interacts with AI daily. Unlocking your smartphone first thing in the morning might require AI-based facial recognition for security. Asking Apple's Siri or Amazon's Alexa for a weather report means tapping into AI. On the drive to work, your car might warn you, via AI sensors, that you are edging too close to another vehicle. If you stop for coffee, you might order on an AI-powered drive-through kiosk. Once at the office, AI apps can help you set your schedule, manage meetings, and review a summary of a conference call. A filing app can retrieve a digital file and locate the sales information your supervisor requested. Chatbots using large language models can generate ideas for client presentations, including graphics and text. You might try two different prompts, one conventional and one a bit off-center, just to check the possibilities. At midmorning your phone's Google Nest doorbell app, powered by AI, shows you that a package was just delivered to your front porch—that mystery novel a coworker recommended. You can also program your air-conditioning unit to ensure your home is cool when you return in the evening.

Many employment experts have warned that adopting AI could reshape the workplace in a negative way for workers. They

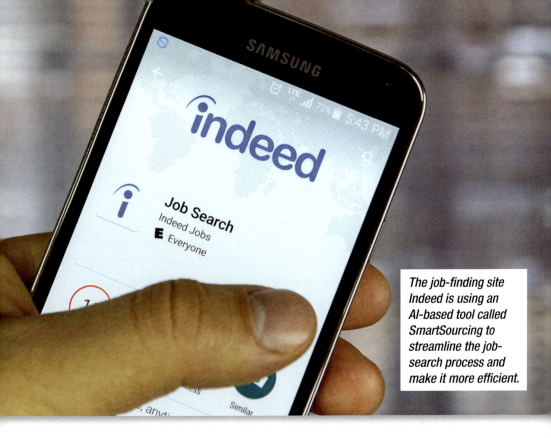

The job-finding site Indeed is using an AI-based tool called SmartSourcing to streamline the job-search process and make it more efficient.

predict that automation with AI stands to eliminate millions of jobs. A March 2023 report from the investment firm Goldman Sachs found that about two-thirds of current jobs are subject to some AI-based automation. Generative AI platforms, like ChatGPT, could take over as much as one-fourth of workplace tasks. Goldman Sachs estimates that GenAI alone could eliminate 300 million full-time jobs globally.

However, others reject such gloomy forecasts. They believe the benefits of AI adoption will outweigh the drawbacks. Although AI might replace certain rote tasks such as data entry, it more often will serve as an assistant in getting things done. For example, many users have testified to AI's value as a source for brainstorming ideas. This can kick-start a worker who otherwise would be stuck wasting valuable time. A user on Reddit with the handle im-Kranely sees AI as a nudge to get the creative juices flowing. According to this user, "By no means is it a replacement for research or creativity, but it's a great tool for when you just need to work through an idea or when you get a bit of mental block."[5] In fact, the names for some popular GenAI platforms—such as Google Assistant and Microsoft Copilot—seem to stress their value as virtual coworkers instead of replacements.

Using AI to Assist with Writing Computer Code

Generative AI platforms promise to revolutionize software development by taking on the task of writing coherent computer code. In early 2024 Alphabet tested its AlphaCode AI model against human coders for speed and accuracy. Engineers found that AlphaCode performed roughly as well as a novice programmer with up to a year of training. "It's not bad at all for an AI," says Bernard Marr, author of *Generative AI in Practice*. "Given that generative AI's capabilities are progressing so fast, we can expect the technology to catch up with more experienced developers in the not-so-distant future."[6]

Using AI for generating code has several advantages. For example, it can start by producing a list of desired outcomes that the user wants the programming code to achieve. AI can then write the code more rapidly than its human counterparts. It can also scan already written code to find errors. It can even suggest changes or improvements in lines of code or predict possible system failures as the work proceeds. Finally, because it responds to prompts in plain language, AI enables those who lack code-writing skills to generate code on their own. AI can also translate code from one computer language to another. Coders at the software firm Freshworks have found that writing code with ChatGPT reduces development time from nine weeks to less than one. A study by the software company GitHub found that its Copilot AI tool enabled developers to code 55 percent faster than before.

> "By no means is it a replacement for research or creativity, but it's a great tool for when you just need to work through an idea or when you get a bit of mental block."[5]
>
> —imKranely, an AI user on Reddit

Adding AI as an Assistant in Computer Coding

"So does this mean we won't need human software developers in the future? No, I don't believe so. But it does mean they will increasingly work alongside AI, just as other professionals will. . . . Admittedly, the work of junior coders could potentially be at risk as more development tasks are automated by AI. However, I see an even bigger application of generative AI than simply automating the work that junior coders would otherwise do. I see generative AI adding enormous value as a copilot or co-coder for even the most experienced programmers."

—Bernard Marr, author of *Generative AI in Practice*

Bernard Marr, "Generative AI Can Write Computer Code. Will We Still Need Software Developers?," *Forbes*, June 7, 2024. www.forbes.com.

Launching Major Changes to Health Care

AI-based solutions are bringing major changes to doctor's offices, hospitals, and health care clinics. For example, doctors have become increasingly distracted during patient visits by having to enter notes into electronic medical records. A new smartphone technology called ambient AI listens in to each visit and transcribes the conversation. Then the app uses machine learning to summarize the clinical content and make draft notes. This allows a doctor to focus on the patient's responses and interact more effectively. The Permanente Medical Group in California reported that, in the first ten weeks that ambient AI was available, 3,442 physicians used it in 303,266 patient visits. Such a high rate of adoption for a new technology shows great promise. Doctors claim that the app saves them as much as an hour a day at the keyboard. "People were genuinely surprised with the ability of the technology to appropriately filter the conversation from a transcript into a clinical note,"[7] says Kristine Lee, an internist and associate executive director of technology and innovation at the Permanente Medical Group.

AI can often interpret diagnostic images with greater accuracy than a human radiologist. In computed tomography (CT) lung scans for cancer screening, a common failure is high rates of false positives and false negatives. A false positive can lead to an unnecessary biopsy when no cancer is present. But a false negative can be deadly, missing signs of cancer on an otherwise normal-looking CT scan. A study published in *Nature Medicine* found that AI analysis of CT lung scans was remarkably accurate at detecting early cancer. The AI even outperformed the radiologists.

Sometimes, a patient's medical condition can baffle experienced doctors. A platform like GPT-4, the latest large language model (LLM) created by OpenAI, has shown promise in correcting a faulty diagnosis or suggesting a rare ailment that had not been considered. Generative AI can access enormous amounts of stored data on medical conditions, including symptoms and side effects of drugs. According to research published in *JAMA Network Open*, GPT-4 provided an accurate diagnosis for four out of six elderly patients with rare conditions. Clinicians, by contrast, correctly diag-

Some AI-based tools help with the process of entering notes, giving doctors more time to focus on patients.

nosed only two of the six. AI assistance is proving to be especially valuable for elderly patients, who may have multiple health problems that complicate diagnosis. Once a diagnosis has been confirmed, AI can also recommend further tests and proper medications.

Bringing Innovation to Law Offices

The legal profession is known for its reliance on tradition. But law offices are already adopting generative AI tools to reduce time spent on rote tasks and boost productivity. An August 2023 survey by data analytics firm LexisNexis found that 50 percent of American lawyers expect AI to transform their practice in significant ways. Not only licensed attorneys but law clerks, paralegals, and secretaries are sure to feel the effects.

Sixty-five percent of lawyers told the LexisNexis survey that they expect research to be AI's chief benefit to law firms. AI can certainly save time by searching through mountains of regulations and case law to find useful precedents. Its findings can rapidly be summarized and placed in a format for further discussion. AI can also check legal briefs for errors, draft legal documents such as trusts and wills, and write and send emails to clients. Use of AI chatbots in law offices is a game-changing move for legal staffers, say Tom Shepherd and Stephanie Lomax of Thomson Reuters Advisory Services. "Large law firms will seek to capture more revenue by deploying staff, including juniors, to higher value work," they note. "Meanwhile, small- and midsize law firms will be able to use Gen AI to grow their practice without needing to hire more staff."[8]

Revolutionizing Warehouse Management and Supply Chains

In today's world of e-commerce, managing warehousing and inventory has become a crucial part of company success. AI systems are already helping automate routine inventory tasks, including order placement, reordering, and expansion. But now companies are unleashing AI's potential to revolutionize the

AI systems can be used to help manage warehousing and inventory. AI has helped automate many routine tasks like this.

warehouse in other ways. The technology is especially adept at using vast amounts of data to improve inventory management. Such data includes inventory levels, sales trends, and seasonal changes. AI can process data with speed and accuracy to align warehouse supply with customer demand and prevent over- or understocking problems. With a constant input of relevant data for machine learning, AI systems can even forecast market conditions and adjust production schedules and inventory accordingly.

Economists have long predicted that adopting AI solutions would drastically reduce jobs related to warehousing and inventory. However, for workers with AI-related skills, many new jobs are being created. For example, AI systems can analyze data for patterns and trends that are often too subtle for humans to see. Nonetheless, the expertise of supply chain managers and their staff is needed to figure out what these trends mean and how to take advantage of them. This involves human decisions about inventory levels and timelines for production and shipping. "In the supply chain industry, AI is already being used to automate tasks such as demand forecasting, inventory management, and optimization," says Maaz Khan, who blogs about supply chain issues.

"By using AI to handle these tasks, supply chain managers can free up their time to focus on more strategic tasks that require human decision-making and creativity."[9]

Another way that supply chain workers can collaborate with AI is by using robotic process automation (RPA) for processing orders. RPA technology handles repetitive tasks such as data entry and invoice processing, enabling workers to make last-minute changes and address customer service issues. To get the most out of working with AI solutions like RPA, employees must be willing to upgrade their knowledge and skills in the technology. It is important for them to regard this learning as an ongoing process. Companies are finding that in-house programs for AI training are an excellent investment.

> "AI is triggering a revolution in what workers can achieve and how valuable they can be to employers. Young people are ideally placed to take advantage of this opportunity and reap the benefits."[10]
>
> —The World Economic Forum

Growing Opportunities for Young Workers

From sifting through résumés to solving supply chain issues, AI continues to impact the workplace for thousands of companies. The ability of GenAI to gather and process data almost instantly makes it an essential tool for law offices and medical clinics. Keeping up with this rapidly changing technology will help young workers stay relevant in the modern workplace. "AI is triggering a revolution in what workers can achieve and how valuable they can be to employers," says an analysis by the World Economic Forum. "Young people are ideally placed to take advantage of this opportunity and reap the benefits."[10]

CHAPTER TWO

Jobs and Careers in AI

The recent boom in AI-related businesses has sent the stock market skyward, but one company's rise has been especially meteoric. Nvidia, which makes high-end computer chips that power generative AI platforms like OpenAI's ChatGPT, saw its stock price explode in 2024. In fact, on June 18 Nvidia's market value exceeded its closest competitors, Microsoft and Apple, making it the most valuable company in the world. On that day, it was worth more than $3.3 trillion. That's trillion with a T. Although its market cap subsequently pulled back some, Nvidia remains one of the biggest success stories in the tech industry. And success of that magnitude leads to job opportunities—lots of them. In fact, tech industry experts are comparing Nvidia's recruiting frenzy to the heyday of Facebook's growth in 2014.

Jensen Huang, CEO of California-based Nvidia, knows that hiring and recruitment are key to his company maintaining its dominant position. Huang says he favors grit and determination over academic credentials when considering job candidates. As he told students at Stanford University, his alma mater, in a March 2024 speech, "Greatness is not intelligence. Greatness comes from character. And character isn't formed out of smart people, it's formed out of people who suffered. . . . To this day I use the phrase 'pain and suffering' inside our company with great glee. I mean that in a happy way, because you want to refine the character of your company. You want greatness out of them."[11] Some might say the word *suffering* goes too far. But Huang wants people who have had to struggle to succeed by overcoming hardships. They should view setbacks as a challenge, not a discouragement. That, he believes, is essential for success.

Looking for Driven, Passionate Employees

Whatever the hard knocks in their background, Nvidia recruits are embracing the boom in AI with its substantial pay and promising career path. Explosive demand for Nvidia's chips is providing jobs in AI storage, chip design, deep learning, software engineering, product development, and even programming for self-driving vehicles. According to *Wall Street Journal* tech analyst Isabelle Bousquette, the company listed more than eighteen hundred job openings in February 2024, with pay ranging from $144,000 to $414,000 a year. Bousquette says the company's roughly thirty thousand employees see themselves as a special group. She explains:

> "They call themselves Nvidians. Takes a special kind of candidate to work there. They hire a lot of recent grads because they're looking for people with really niche [specialized] knowledge. . . . It's a combination of people who have those skills and are also really, really driven, really passionate."[12]
>
> —Isabelle Bousquette, tech analyst at the *Wall Street Journal*

> They call themselves Nvidians. Takes a special kind of candidate to work there. They hire a lot of recent grads because they're looking for people with really niche [specialized] knowledge. . . . It's a combination of people who have those skills and are also really, really driven, really passionate. Some former employees describe it as almost like a startup culture, very intense, a lot of pressure to sort of get things done, innovate quickly.[12]

Nvidia also enlists its employees in the search for new talent. They know from their daily work what kind of candidates are most valuable, with strong character traits and technical skills. More than 39 percent of the company's hires come from employee referrals.

Workers can earn bonuses if they refer someone who ends up getting hired. Offering such incentives means that the entire workforce at Nvidia can play a role in recruitment. Huang sees this as necessary due to the fierce competition in AI and its related companies. Established chip makers Intel and AMD are also in hot pursuit of personnel with high potential. Meanwhile, tech giants Google, Apple, and Amazon are developing their own specialized AI-related chips. For example, Google wants its chip designers to focus on areas such as YouTube advertising and data analysis. The hope is that chips created in-house will reduce Google's reliance on outside vendors and boost the company's efforts to incorporate AI. Developers with fresh ideas are essential for such a push.

Amid surging interest in generative AI, a company like Nvidia is more willing to take chances on new employees. "Again, here is a good place to take note of how Nvidia operates," says John Kim of Paraform, which connects tech businesses with recruits. "The company hires extremely experienced leadership, but takes more liberties when recruiting entry-level staff. Too risky to hire an untried CFO [chief financial officer], for example—but hiring an authentically strange backend developer [to write code for an AI app]? The downside is limited, and the upside is immense."[13]

The recent boom in AI-related businesses has caused a huge increase in the value of stock for Nvidia, which makes high-end computer chips that power generative AI platforms.

The Importance of AI Skills in the Job Marketplace

For all sorts of jobs in today's business world, it pays to have AI skills. Industries are integrating AI into their daily operations at a record pace. Ongoing advancements in the technology have made AI tools and platforms attractive for their accuracy, efficiency, and cost-saving potential. AI already can do many tasks once considered the exclusive province of human workers, such as answering customer service calls and managing warehouse inventory. Nearly 70 percent of corporate leaders say they will no longer hire applicants without some level of AI skills. They would rather hire a less-experienced candidate with these skills than a more-experienced person without them.

Personnel managers are looking to hire a wide range of AI workers, from novices in the technology to experts with specialized, cutting edge skills. Although tech companies lead the way in AI hiring, consulting firms and health care companies also offer lots of job opportunities. On average, the business-focused social network LinkedIn lists more than fifteen thousand AI-related jobs every day. Once an employee has landed a job working with AI, it is important to stay current (as much as possible) on trends and innovations in the technology.

Certain jobs in AI are in strong demand and seem certain to remain that way. These generally call for technical skills in data analysis and programming. For example, machine-learning (ML) engineers design, develop, and implement AI systems that employ large data sets for machine learning. They generate algorithms that enable the system to learn and make predictions. More than 60 percent of ML engineers have a background in computer science or engineering. They understand common computer languages like Java, Python, and C++, as well as less-used ones like Lisp and Prolog.

A successful ML engineer tends to be curious, efficient, and good at problem solving. This person must rapidly sift through large data sets and be able to identify hidden patterns, whether

Job Opportunities in AI Infrastructure

The massive rollout of AI technology promises to offer lots of job opportunities in infrastructure. Outfitting data centers to employ AI requires major upgrades to handle the larger workloads. Planners and tech workers are needed to retrofit existing data centers with graphics processing units and other AI hardware. In addition, many vast new data centers are being planned, with investments in the billions. Powering these data centers presents more challenges. Experts in power generation, electricity grids, and cooling systems stand to become essential in the new AI-dominated tech landscape. They must find cost-effective ways to expand the electrical grid and satisfy the power supply demands of the new technology.

through logic or intuition. Anne Nies, director of machine learning at a large data science firm, says creativity is also important for ML engineers. "A lot of the work we're trying to do hasn't been done before so exceptional candidates are creative," says Nies. "Part of creativity is also about being ready to take risks and having the resiliency to try again when those risks don't turn out the way that you expected."[14] ML engineers are being enlisted in all sorts of efforts worldwide, from wildlife conservation in the western United States to exploring for copper and other minerals in Zambia.

Applying AI to Banking and Finance

Another promising career path related to AI awaits in the finance sector. This is where decisions are made about managing money and investments. Such a data-driven industry presents major opportunities for ML engineers, data analysts, and AI consultants as the industry adapts to the new technology. The financial world thrives on historical data to forecast stock market moves, interest rates, and gyrations in the overall economy. AI can find telltale patterns amid the statistical noise and suggest strategies to use those patterns for successful investments.

Credit helps fuel the economy, and decisions on credit have a large effect on how people live. Companies today are seeking employees with AI skills to help banks and other lenders make better and more rapid credit decisions. Los Angeles–based Zest AI manages to include a push for fairness and ethical outcomes in its use of AI credit-check software. For instance, Zest FairBoost mines traditional customer data along with often overlooked data points to help determine a person's genuine credit risk. This helps lenders identify underserved borrowers who may have been misevaluated or overlooked. Such borrowers can then be given new opportunities for loans. "Zest AI has always been ahead of the curve when it comes to fair lending technology," says Sean Kamkar, Zest AI's senior vice president and head of data science. "Zest FairBoost is our way of taking a stand and saying that finding fairer outcomes will always be a priority and that equal access to credit is a job that is never finished."[15]

There is a growing demand for employees who can adapt AI to analyze companies for their investment potential. Research at the University of Chicago Booth School of Business shows that

AI is being used to help some banks make better and more rapid credit decisions for use in determining things like interest rates for home loans.

AI and LLMs can match and even outperform human financial analysts. For the test, OpenAI's GPT-4 used company balance sheets, income statements, and other public information to analyze performance for more than fifteen thousand companies over several decades. The goal was to predict whether earnings would be higher or lower and by what magnitude. The AI platform's predictions were correct 60 percent of the time, compared to just 52 percent for human analysts. As Valeri V. Nikolaev, who led the study, observed, "Given that GPT outperforms human analysts in predicting future earnings, this finding raises the question of whether an LLM can largely replace a median human analyst."[16] Nikolaev noted that it is still important to have a human operator to guide ChatGPT's analysis.

Experience with generative AI platforms can also lead to a career as a compliance expert. Banks, brokerages, real estate firms, and insurance companies must navigate a sea of laws and government regulations in their dealings with clients and other institutions. A compliance expert uses AI to review contracts, real estate deeds, trusts, and wills. This person also checks to see that the company is complying with federal and state laws and regulations. AI can monitor and evaluate data on these issues to detect and flag possible risks. It can also spot new legal requirements that a human analyst might have missed. Armed with AI, a compliance expert can save his or her employers enormous amounts of time and money.

AI Creatives: Careers in Art and Entertainment

For people who thrive on creative work, knowledge of generative AI can open lots of doors. For example, some of the top producers in the $200 billion video game industry are turning to AI to save time and money. Activision, the studio that produces wildly popular games such as *Call of Duty* and *World of Warcraft*, recently began using internal art created through AI apps such

A videographer works on the soundtrack for a film. Generative music platforms can be used to help create musical scores for movies.

as Midjourney and Stable Diffusion. With tons of digital graphic art across the internet at their disposal, these platforms can generate otherworldly landscapes and characters in minutes. Some deplore the fact that traditional artists at these studios are being laid off. However, the changeover means fresh opportunities for applicants with a background in generative AI art. "It's here. It's definitely here, right now," says Violet, a game developer, technical artist, and veteran of the industry for over a decade. "I think everyone's seen it get used, and it's a matter of how and to what degree. The genie is out of the bottle, Pandora's box is opened."[17]

Music-oriented AI chatbots can also contribute to the soundtracks of games and movies. Generative music platforms such as AIVA and Fadr enable AI to create musical scores based on different styles and genres of music—and sometimes a combination of genres in a distinctive mash-up.

> "[AI is] here. It's definitely here, right now. I think everyone's seen it get used, and it's a matter of how and to what degree. The genie is out of the bottle, Pandora's box is opened."[17]
>
> —Violet, a game developer and technical artist

Filmmakers increasingly are looking into AI to mimic the styles of favorite composers. Gareth Edwards, director of *Rogue One: A Star Wars Story*, wanted soundtrack music for another project that suggested the sound of Oscar-winning composer Hans Zimmer. The samples he got from an AI music company rated only 7 on a scale of 10 in Edwards's opinion. He ended up using Zimmer himself for the soundtrack. But tech experts believe that AI-based musical creations are sure to be used in more films and television productions going forward. "From my experience, some quite simple AI music is pretty convincing," says Henry Ajder, a specialist in generative AI. "It's difficult to tell the difference between an AI-generated composition and a human-performed composition."[18] This development bodes well for workers with a background in both music and generative AI.

A Wide-Open Future for Careers in AI

Career opportunities in AI are on the rise in the United States and around the world. Companies like Nvidia make high-end chips that form the backbone of generative AI. They provide jobs for chip designers, software engineers, robotics experts, and testing professionals. Company heads in many industries, from finance to entertainment, agree that AI skills are becoming vital for job applicants. This includes both novices and experienced hands. As the technology continues to develop at a dizzying pace, workers can look forward to a wide-open future for AI-related careers.

CHAPTER THREE

Preparing for a Career in AI

In March 2024, when thirty-one-year-old Asif Dhanani lost his job as a technical product manager at Amazon, he knew that he had to retool his résumé. The job market in the tech industry, he realized, demands AI skills. The Irvine, California, resident has a background in AI but has not worked with LLMs since 2016. Changes to the technology since then have left him unprepared for the new AI landscape. He has landed interviews for product manager but received no concrete job offers. He was concerned when personnel managers said they were sifting through hundreds of applicants. Dhanani also had a feeling that those in charge of hiring were not quite sure themselves what they wanted in an AI-experienced employee. Determined to revive his career, Dhanani paid $6,800 to enroll in a two-week online AI boot camp. He considered the intensive Deep Atlas training course a great investment for building skills. Deep Atlas cofounder Tony Phillips acknowledges the surge in cases like Dhanani's. "People started to see the writing on the wall that their jobs really could be obsolete," he says. "You're probably not going to get replaced by AI. You're going to be replaced by someone who knows AI and does your job."[19]

> "People started to see the writing on the wall that their jobs really could be obsolete. You're probably not going to get replaced by AI. You're going to be replaced by someone who knows AI and does your job."[19]
>
> —Tony Phillips, cofounder of Deep Atlas, a school for AI and machine learning

An Unbalanced Labor Market for AI

Tech veterans like Dhanani are finding themselves caught in a competitive but unbalanced labor market. Candidates for software engineering jobs are easy to find. But companies are desperate to hire tier-one workers with technical knowledge and experience with LLMs. These are the mountains of text that feed the chatbots that generate content. Qualified workers in ChatGPT, Microsoft Copilot, and other generative AI platforms can command six-figure salaries at a minimum. And growing companies seeking to compete with industry leaders are offering eye-popping compensation packages that approach $1 million, including stock options and travel perks. Some are luring away whole teams of LLM specialists from the giants. Databricks, a start-up in data storage and management, focuses its search on LLM experts who can deal with thorny AI issues such as hallucinations—which are flawed or incorrect output. "There is a secular shift in what talents we're going after," says Naveen Rao, who heads Generative AI at Databricks. "We have a glut of people on one side and a shortage on the other."[20] Rao says that salespeople with detailed knowledge of AI are also in high demand and short supply.

With AI-related skills so crucial in today's job market, first-time job seekers and tech veterans alike must prepare themselves for success. Whereas novices need to learn the basics of AI, more experienced workers like Dhanani are finding they must retool their skill sets to revitalize their careers. Many tech companies are focused on making their whole workforce more proficient with AI. Salesforce, a firm that manages customer relations, has an in-house training program with forty-three separate AI courses. The courses cover everything from AI basics to the ethics of using AI. Jayesh Govindarajan, senior vice president of Salesforce AI, views such company-wide efforts as essential. "We believe that everyone should be reskilled and in some way have the tools they need to succeed in this new world,"[21] he says.

Creating a Strong Basis in AI in High School and College

Tech experts say that a grounding in AI-related skills should begin in high school. Courses in STEM subject areas—science, tech-

AI is having a significant effect on the labor market. With AI-related skills so crucial in today's job market, people looking for a job might want to invest in AI training.

nology, engineering, and mathematics—create a strong basis for a career in AI. Classes in statistics, programming, and computer science are excellent preparatory sources. In a computer science class, students can learn about app development, web design, machine learning, neural networks, and animation. Some high schools have technology specialists that work with single-subject STEM teachers to show how AI concepts are connected to other disciplines.

In fact, many experts believe that high school curricula should include elements of AI education for everyone. Even students who have no plans to work with AI can benefit from learning the basics of the technology. AI is already transforming industries and helping reshape society. Students who understand AI concepts will enjoy a competitive edge in fields as diverse as data science, cybersecurity, finance, marketing, energy, research, and health care. Almost any career path going forward is likely to touch on AI solutions in some way.

Surveys indicate that high school students tend to be wary of artificial intelligence—even more so than their parents or teachers. A 2023 survey from the Walton Family Foundation found that teachers are more likely to use ChatGPT than their students, by a 63 percent to 42 percent margin. Many students see AI mainly as a threat to jobs and thus an omen of an uncertain future. "While educators fret about plagiarism, cheating, and how to use AI to improve instruction, students are wrestling with more fundamental questions about what they are learning and why," says Michael B. Horn, executive editor of *Education Next*. "They are looking at the fast-changing world and wondering if their coursework is properly preparing them for the workplaces of tomorrow."[22]

Educators are hearing these concerns and acting to address them. Martin West, academic dean at the Harvard Graduate School of Education, urges high school teachers to worry less about students cheating on book reports with AI. Teachers should concentrate instead on class assignments and learning goals that emphasize AI's potential. He suggests that assignments be redesigned so that students gain experience in applying AI in useful ways. He also believes that using AI for classwork should not only be permitted but encouraged. West notes that Harvard faculty are already adopting these ideas to prepare their students for today's professional world.

AI is altering the landscape for college degrees as well. A growing number of universities offer four-year degree programs in AI. It still helps to obtain a degree in computer science or information technology to prepare for a career in AI. But today's college courses offer more chances for specialization, such as machine learning, data analytics, and advanced robotics. And, says Maria Flynn, president and chief executive of Jobs for the Future, college students should not neglect nontechnical skills that enhance their value to employers. As Flynn notes, "It's important that AI degrees and other education training programs not only focus on specific skill development, but that the focus is on helping students learn how to learn, which includes developing an intellectual curiosity,

> ### Writing Effective Prompts
>
> Banjaxed Solutions, a tech partner of Salesforce, offers tips for writing effective AI prompts:
>
> > Be specific and detailed. The more precise you are when you talk to AI, the more precise your results will be. . . .
>
> > Use clear, concise language. . . . When you talk to AI bots, keep your question to the point and [be] specific. . . .
>
> > Avoid overly complex or open-ended questions. Simple is better. . . .
>
> > Describe a preferred complexity of response. As you talk to AI . . . [use] phrases such as "explain to me as if I were a CEO" or "as if I were a 5th grader."
>
> Bec Morris, "Chatting with Chatbots—How to Talk to AI," Banjaxed Solutions. www.banjaxed.com.

and skills like leadership, communication and critical thinking."[23] Programs are also placing an emphasis on adapting AI skills for the changing job market, including at non-tech companies. Many colleges have ties to companies that offer internship programs. Although competition for these slots is intense, an internship at a company that is rapidly integrating AI into its workplace can jump-start a graduate's career.

Introductory Courses and Online AI Boot Camps

The best way to improve job prospects in AI is to acquire technical knowledge and skills. Workers new to AI should consider taking an online course to learn the technology's basics. Those with a background in this technology can benefit from refresher courses that explore the latest developments in generative AI and related areas. "The importance of learning technical skills cannot be understated," says Michael Stedman, digital marketing specialist at Yoh Services, a talent and staffing source for tech companies.

"The bottom line is that candidates with the required technical skills will outshine those without. . . . Therefore, it's your responsibility to research what technical skills are expected of each role to build your skillset accordingly."[24]

A good place to start is an online course that presents the fundamental ideas behind AI. Online platforms such as Udacity, edX, and Coursera offer courses that are created in conjunction with pros at leading tech companies. Udacity's Introduction to Artificial Intelligence, for example, explains the basic concepts of AI in plain language. The user learns how to set up a programming environment and work on AI problems with Python or other computer languages. One lesson has the user apply AI to solve sudoku puzzles. Many high schools and colleges recommend that their students take one of these introductory online courses.

For more comprehensive, practical training, an online AI boot camp is an excellent resource. A typical AI boot camp deals with machine learning, data science, LLMs, and other AI-related do-

Experts say that teens should start learning AI skills in high school. Courses in STEM subject areas—science, technology, engineering, and mathematics—create a strong basis for a career in AI.

mains. Tech workers like Asif Dhanani use boot camps as refresher courses to learn the latest cutting edge AI skills. Online boot camps can last anywhere from two weeks to several months depending on the level of skills instruction. They are not cheap, as demonstrated by the $6,800 tuition fee Dhanani paid for a Deep Atlas two-week boot camp. However, many boot camps offer installment plans for payment. Some have scholarships or loans for students in need. Some boot camps also offer job guarantees, with a full refund of the tuition if a student is unable to get an industry job within a certain period. These guarantees affirm that online AI boot camps expect to produce job-ready candidates for AI-related positions. Many boot camps are affiliated with tech companies and enlist learners to work on actual company projects using AI and machine learning.

Another option for employees seeking to improve their AI skills is to take in-house training courses. Surprisingly, despite increased spending on AI, not enough companies in the United States are investing in their own workers' training. Only 38 percent of executives say they are helping their workforce learn AI skills on the job. However, some tech firms are offering tutorials in generative AI as a perk to attract employees. "If . . . you're trying to attract job candidates who want to continuously build their digital skills, promising them training in GenAI should be a no-brainer," says Allison Horn, executive director for consulting firm Accenture. "The same goes for making GenAI training available to existing employees as a retention tool."[25]

Building AI Skills with Prompt Practice

One surefire way for office workers to boost their value to a company is to develop skills in generative AI. And the key skill to unlocking AI's potential is prompt engineering. In simple terms, this means writing prompts that chatbots can understand and that will get the desired results. Writing effective prompts for ChatGPT or Microsoft Copilot can take hours of practice, with lots of trial and error. But like explaining office procedures to a new coworker, it takes patience to find the right approach. *Wall Street Journal* tech reporter Bart Ziegler says it also requires some imagination:

> Want to get the best answers out of an AI? It's all in how you talk to it. Tell it, for instance, to pretend it is Albert Einstein. Or that somebody's life depends on the response. Or that it needs to stay focused on its goals. Prodding an artificial-intelligence chatbot is nothing like doing a Google search. Instead, it is like having a conversation with a book-smart person who needs coaxing—sometimes very indirect or bizarre coaxing—to give the most creative and effective answers to questions. The trouble is, nobody knows why AI responds to those strange prompts in the ways it does—not even the people who created large language models such as OpenAI's ChatGPT, Google's Gemini and Microsoft's Copilot. That has led to experiments and guesswork to find the approaches that work best. Some researchers even ask the chatbots themselves for tips on how to talk to them.[26]

Microsoft researchers have also learned that chatbots deliver an improved response when told that a bad result could cost the user their job. A test of more than two hundred high-difficulty language-based tasks showed chatbots performed 115 percent better when prodded with urgent messages. In their study, the Microsoft researchers found that chatbots "possess emotional intelligence and can be enhanced by emotional stimuli."[27] Encouraging words also seem to help. Users who told the chatbot to take a deep breath and work through the problem step-by-step got better results from their prompts. Once engaged as a trusted assistant, a chatbot—like most workers—seems to warm to its task.

> "Want to get the best answers out of an AI? It's all in how you talk to it. Tell it, for instance, to pretend it is Albert Einstein. Or that somebody's life depends on the response. Or that it needs to stay focused on its goals."[26]
>
> —Bart Ziegler, tech reporter for the *Wall Street Journal*

Developing generative AI skills is one way for office workers to increase their value. However, writing effective prompts for ChatGPT can take hours of practice, with lots of trial and error.

An Automated Assistant for the Future

Whether starting or maintaining a career in AI, workers must be open to constant learning of AI-related skills. Experienced tech workers are finding it necessary to enroll in online AI boot camps for an intensive refresher course midcareer. Novice employees can take online courses that explain the basic concepts of the technology in plain language. Experimenting with GenAI and writing prompts helps individuals develop reliable skills. Workers also are learning that AI offers many practical benefits for everyday tasks. These include tracking meetings, managing email, and streamlining repetitive jobs like invoicing and budgeting. For long-term success, workers should embrace AI as an automated assistant for the future.

CHAPTER FOUR

Challenges of Working with AI

On February 6, 2023, Google launched an online GIF advertisement on X to demonstrate the practical abilities of its new chatbot, Bard. The ad showed how Bard could help parents or students answer questions using AI and LLMs. One prompt asked, "What new discoveries from the James Webb Space Telescope (JWST) can I tell my 9-year old about?"[28] One of Bard's answers claimed that the JWST had taken the first pictures of an exoplanet, or a planet outside Earth's solar system. However, as astrophysicist Grant Tremblay was quick to point out—and the National Aeronautics and Space Administration (NASA) confirmed—this response was incorrect. The first pictures of exoplanets were taken by the European Southern Observatory's Very Large Telescope in 2004.

Well, one might say, everyone makes mistakes. Even a highly touted conversational chatbot. But this mistake proved especially costly for Google's parent company, Alphabet, and its investors. When the stock market opened the next day, Alphabet stock dropped more than 9 percent and lost $100 billion in value. Tech experts chided Google for rushing Bard's debut and staging such a high-profile failure—and just when it was trying to prove Bard's superiority to OpenAI's ChatGPT, the industry leader. Bard not only was sent back for further testing, it also wound up with a name change, to Google Gemini. In a later tweet, Tremblay praised Google for bringing attention to the space telescope. However, he could not resist adding, "But ChatGPT etc., while spooky impressive, are often *very confidently* wrong. Will be interesting to see a future where LLMs self error check."[29]

Potential for Errors and Hallucinations

Tremblay was pointing out one of the main problems with generative AI: its potential to make mistakes. This becomes especially risky for users when a chatbot from Microsoft or Google is used as a search engine. Instead of answering queries by drawing on a database of proven facts, a chatbot is trained to look for patterns in mountains of text. These patterns help it decide how to build sentences word by word on any topic. But they do not necessarily assure that the sentences are based on facts. Chatbots quite often produce structurally well-written material that nonetheless contains errors—sometimes lots of them.

In May 2024 a storm arose in the media over Google's new AI-based search engine, called AI Overviews. Workers began posting examples of the chatbot's misinformation, such as saying that a dog once played in the National Hockey League. It also offered advice that was not only wrong but dangerous. AI Overviews listed the health benefits of running with scissors, recommended adding glue to spaghetti sauce for thickness, and suggested that people should eat one small rock every day. (These responses were apparently picked up from satirical humor sites.) A disclaimer at the bottom of each AI Overviews answer, noting that generative AI is experimental, did little to calm the critics.

When a chatbot's response to a question is incorrect or misleading, it is called a hallucination. Such a response is presented as a solid fact, often making it difficult to recognize as a mistake. Tech experts consider hallucinations to be the biggest problem with AI tools. They can be caused by insufficient or low-quality data, poor data-retrieval systems, or badly written prompts. Chatbots have even fabricated kings and countries that never existed.

Dealing with AI Errors at Work

Employees who depend on generative AI in the workplace need to constantly be on the lookout for this type of malfunction. Examples from AI Overviews may sound absurd, but hallucinations, if not spotted in time, can have serious consequences. Attorneys have submitted AI-assisted legal briefs that referred to court cases that were completely made up. Patients who ask a chatbot for advice on medical treatment can receive misguided suggestions that endanger their health. Technicians at OpenAI, Google, and Microsoft are working feverishly to eliminate hallucinations. They have created tools and guardrails to make certain kinds of errors much less likely to occur. For example, one tool gives an AI platform access to a specific database that includes the correct information needed for doing its job.

As a worker, there are steps you can take to prevent hallucinations. Write prompts in clear language that calls for one operation only. This will reduce the chance that the AI will go astray. Do not use a chatbot designed for general use, like ChatGPT, for profes-

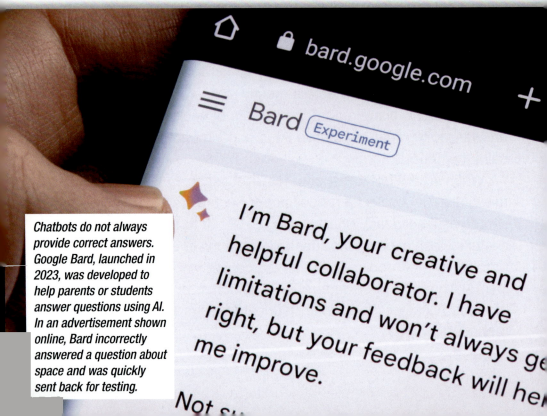

Chatbots do not always provide correct answers. Google Bard, launched in 2023, was developed to help parents or students answer questions using AI. In an advertisement shown online, Bard incorrectly answered a question about space and was quickly sent back for testing.

sional content like case law or scientific theories. Any answers the AI provides regarding specialist material are likely to be flawed. Also, provide as much context as you can in your prompts. This will help guide the AI tool to the right information sources. And be sure to fact-check AI responses that have the most practical impact. If the chatbot says early voting begins in a state on a certain day, check that state's election schedule to corroborate this detail.

> "No matter how careful you are, expect any AI tool you use to occasionally just get weird. If you expect the occasional hallucination or wild response, you can catch them before your AI chatbot gets your company brought to court."[30]
>
> —Harry Guinness, a blogger at Zapier

Ultimately, experts say, AI users must accept that hallucinations occur. "No matter how careful you are, expect any AI tool you use to occasionally just get weird," says Harry Guinness, a blogger at Zapier, which makes automated workflow software. "If you expect the occasional hallucination or wild response, you can catch them before your AI chatbot gets your company brought to court."[30]

Alert to Bias and Discrimination

AI systems are only as reliable as the data sets they tap into, and flaws in the data sets can carry over to AI responses. Working with AI tools can produce results that are biased against groups that historically have suffered from discrimination. These include people of color, women, people with disabilities, and the LGBTQ community. If the data a chatbot accesses is biased in some way, the AI algorithms will reproduce the bias. The hazard increases when AI is sifting through older data and news stories that do not reflect current standards of fairness and inclusion. Therefore, AI users in the workplace should always be alert to evidence of bias and discrimination, however subtle it might be.

AI engineers at IBM point to several common instances of bias in AI. In health care, data covering women or minorities often is underrepresented in AI, thus skewing its algorithms and producing biased results. AI tracking systems for job applicants may process language in ways that discriminate. For example, Amazon's AI hiring software favored résumés with words such as *executed* or *captured*, which were found more often on men's applications. Google's chatbot for online advertising showed males in highly paid positions more often than women. The AI art app Midjourney, when asked to provide images of people in professions such as law or medicine, always depicted the older people as male. Law enforcement officials say AI policing tools used to predict high-crime areas may be based on outdated arrest data. This can perpetuate racial profiling and discrimination in policing.

Biased results in AI can also be inadvertent and hard to detect. The French pharmaceutical company Sanofi is addressing this problem in developing its own AI systems. Lionel Bascles, head of clinical sciences and operations at Sanofi, notes:

> Unlike conscious bias, unconscious biases are difficult to capture at the start (design phase) of AI product development, but they might be discovered once the AI system[s] are put into practice (operational phase). Knowing this, we intend to tackle this by monitoring AI systems to remain vigilant of risks, capture any unknown biases, and to put a mitigation plan into action to maintain compliance with strict standards.[31]

Tech experts note that some forms of bias are built into AI systems because their creators have such a narrow perspective. Of the world's more than seven thousand natural languages, for example, only one hundred have been used to train the leading chatbots. This also explains why AI programs for speech recognition so often fail to understand certain speech dialects and accents.

Deepfakes and Deliberate Deception

A major fear that social critics have about AI involves deliberate deception. GenAI enables bad actors to create so-called deep-

AI allows the creation of deepfakes, which can be hard to distinguish from the real thing. This picture shows an example of deepfake technology, where facial features in an image are changed but still resemble the same person.

fakes, which are fake images, videos, or audio clips that are difficult to distinguish from the real thing. AI-based voice changers can mimic the speech of celebrities or politicians with startling accuracy. Anyone working with AI tools should be wary of deceptive output at every stage of a project.

AI's growing capacity to produce remarkably detailed fake material raises the stakes for misinformation, propaganda, and inflammatory claims. Concerned observers from Pope Francis to United Nations secretary-general António Guterres have warned that AI deceptions spread by social media may be a threat to peace and democracy. A June 2024 report on AI from former UK prime minister Tony Blair and a conservative colleague urged governments to set up safeguards to combat deepfakes. Some social critics believe we are hurtling toward a time when people start to lose trust on a massive scale. "No one knows what's real and what's not," says Martin Ford, a futurist and technology expert. "You literally cannot believe your

Asking AI to Eliminate the Bias

Confronted with the problem of Western cultural bias in AI outputs, researchers at the Technical University of Darmstadt in Germany came up with a novel solution. They simply asked the AI model for answers that were less biased. Working with the AI start-up Hugging Face, the research team came up with a tool they called Fair Diffusion. It allows users to adjust AI models to get the diverse types of images they prefer. For example, Fair Diffusion takes AI-generated stock photos of CEOs in various backgrounds and replaces the White men with images of females or people of color.

own eyes and ears; you can't rely on what, historically, we've considered to be the best possible evidence. . . . That's going to be a huge issue."[32]

Ethical Issues with Generative AI

Those who work with GenAI every day must also deal with its related ethical issues. As chatbots comb through cyberspace picking up data in response to prompts, they are liable to trespass on copyrighted material. This includes writing, photographs, musical compositions, artwork, and other intellectual property. Even licensed computer code has allegedly been plundered. Recently, artists and photographers have begun filing lawsuits against AI platforms that they accuse of poaching their images. GenAI creates its models by training artificial neural networks on enormous tracts of data, including images. According to legal claims, AI art programs like DeviantArt, Midjourney, and Stability AI train their models by using copyrighted images without the creators' consent. Getty Images

> "[Concerning deepfakes,] no one knows what's real and what's not. You literally cannot believe your own eyes and ears; you can't rely on what, historically, we've considered to be the best possible evidence. . . . That's going to be a huge issue."[32]
>
> —Martin Ford, a futurist and technology expert

is suing Stability AI for alleged copyright infringement in its use of more than 12 million photographs and captions in its image training. No binding standard has yet been established for creative materials produced by AI, and the legal landscape remains murky and uncertain. Courts are likely to be addressing the issue for years to come. However, users of GenAI should be aware of the possibility for copyright violations. Companies such as Microsoft have already started removing copyrighted material from their AI training data.

A related question is whether works created with AI can be copyrighted. The purpose of a copyright is to allow creators to profit from their works, thus encouraging creativity. But since AI algorithms do not require such incentives, the US Copyright Office has ruled that AI-created works are not eligible for copyright. By the same token, people who write AI prompts are unlikely to be granted

A woman creates images with Midjourney, which is an AI art program. Critics have charged that programs like this train their models by using copyrighted images without the creators' consent.

copyright protections for their work. The AI-generated material that results from the prompts is, after all, the random product of LLMs and machine learning. "Where does this leave us? For the moment, in limbo," say Kate Crawford and Jason Schultz, professors in tech research and law respectively. "The billions of works produced by generative AI are unowned and can be used anywhere, by anyone, for any purpose. . . . This is a radical moment in creative production: a stream of works without any legally recognizable author."[33]

Ethical questions also have arisen about AI's violations of personal privacy. While trolling for data in far corners of the internet, AI chatbots are liable to collect personal data, including financial or employment information, without the owner's knowledge. Users should be careful about offering any personal information in a prompt. OpenAI recently equipped ChatGPT with a feature that allows users to prevent the chatbot from saving their inputs for training. However, most users are not even aware that their data might be stored to shape future responses. Workers in health care or medical insurance have to be especially alert to exposing patients' personal data to AI platforms and training algorithms. More companies today are educating staff members on safe and ethical use of AI chatbots. Such programs include what kind of data can and cannot be used safely as inputs for GenAI.

A Host of Problems and Challenges

Not long ago, most workers would have said the biggest drawback to AI is its potential to take their jobs. But more widespread use of generative AI has revealed that the technology has its own problems and presents many challenges. Workers must constantly look out for errors and hallucinations; examples of bias and discrimination; deliberately deceptive outputs, such as deepfakes; and ethical problems with unauthorized use of copyrighted materials and personal data. Whether these problems are a permanent fixture or can be eliminated in later versions of AI tools remains to be seen.

CHAPTER FIVE

A Bright Future for a New Technology

The Mars rover that explored the surface of the Red Planet beginning in February 2021 is called *Perseverance*. That name also fits Vandi Verma, its main architect. For more than twenty years, Verma has been designing and building robots for space exploration, especially for missions to Mars. As chief engineer for robotic operations at NASA, she employs AI at every stage of creation. In fact, AI is the main source of *Perseverance*'s ability to think, navigate, and handle samples while operating 140 million miles (225 million km) from Earth. *Percy*, as Verma and her engineers call the intrepid car-sized rover, in many ways has a mind of its own.

AI technology also allows Verma and her team to improve the rover's systems as the mission is proceeding. "While we can't upgrade the hardware while it's up there, we can upgrade the software," she says. "We've done three software upgrades since we landed. We add new capabilities, test them, and figure out how we're going to use them. That's all part of the work."[34] Verma says the AI upgrades help *Percy* make decisions such as what rocks are most worthy of study. AI also enables the rover to do several things at once, while also calculating the energy needed to complete each task. "So that's where I think the huge change is," she says. "The capability and the trust are to the point where we've seen over time enough correct decisions by the AI that we are now willing to let it take control."[35]

New Jobs Powered by Advances in AI

Operating a Mars rover like *Perseverance* seems like a dream job to many tech-oriented people. But breakthroughs in AI, like the ones Verma is making with NASA's smart rover, promise to spur all sorts of new and interesting jobs in the future. Moreover, AI advances in one industry tend to spread rapidly to others, providing even more opportunities.

> "So that's where I think the huge change is. . . . The capability and the trust are to the point where we've seen over time enough correct decisions by the AI that we are now willing to let it take control."[35]
>
> —Vandi Verma, chief engineer for robotic operations at NASA

An example of this is the cutting edge AI technology called digital twins. In September 2020, NASA engineers debuted *Percy*'s full-size earthbound replica, named *OPTIMISM*. This digital double is designed to test all the tricky maneuvers that *Percy* must perform. For example, *OPTIMISM*'s first major test was a simulated landing maneuver called Skycrane. For the test, which was conducted virtually via OPTIMISM's onboard computer, a supersonic parachute attached to a rocket-powered crane successfully lowered the rover to the ground by way of nylon cables. What engineers learned from the computer test was transferred to *Percy*'s software. Weeks later, Verma and her team at NASA's Jet Propulsion Laboratory (JPL) held their breath as *Percy* plummeted toward the Martian landscape at high speed. They referred to the seven-minute delay in communications as the "seven minutes of terror."[36] But *Percy* made it through the perilous Skycrane landing on Mars with no problem.

After the Skycrane test, *OPTIMISM* made a series of trial runs on a rock-strewn California mock-up of Mars. AI-based data from these test runs helped *Percy* navigate its way over the slopes and craters of the genuine Red Planet. "The size and shape of rocks in the visual field—will they turn into obstacles or not?" says

This NASA illustration depicts the Perseverance rover operating on the surface of Mars. The rover's creator has been building robots for space exploration for more than twenty years and uses AI at every stage of creation.

Bryan Martin, flight software manager at JPL. "We test a lot of that, figure out what kinds of things to avoid. What we have safely traversed around here has informed rover drivers in planning their traverses on Mars. We've done so much testing on the ground we can be confident in it. It works."[37]

The digital twins concept works so well that it is being adopted in industries as diverse as manufacturing and health care. Manufacturers use it to test the performance of machines and equipment. Sensors powered by AI send data about each machine in real time to its digital twin. The twin can help forecast breakdowns and predict when maintenance will be required. It can also process data about force and friction that increase tool wear and then take steps to correct the problem. Companies can even create digital twins of the whole factory system. This allows engineers to monitor compliance with regulations and improve how the separate parts work together. The result is lower costs, fewer errors, and better quality.

Using AI to Discover Cognitive Risk Factors

AI may soon play a major role in spotting risk factors for Alzheimer's disease and other forms of dementia. Scientists at the University of California, San Francisco (UCSF), have come up with a method to predict Alzheimer's disease as early as seven years before its symptoms appear. They use AI and machine learning to analyze patient records for signs of risk. "This is a first step towards using AI on routine clinical data," says the study's lead author, Alice Tang, a graduate student at the UCSF lab, "not only to identify risk as early as possible, but also to understand the biology behind it."

Quoted in Victoria Colliver, "How AI Can Help Spot Early Risk Factors for Alzheimer's Disease," UCSF, February 21, 2024. www.ucsf.edu.

In health care, digital twins have countless applications. Digital replicas of tumors enable doctors to test different treatment options and help refine surgical approaches. Dr. Caroline Chung, a radiation oncologist at MD Anderson Cancer Center in Houston, Texas, sees exciting possibilities for creating lifesaving treatments. "Digital twins of individual cells, organs or systems have the potential to inform decisions and to reduce the time and cost of discovering and developing new drugs and therapeutics,"[38] she says. The technology also promises to revolutionize health care systems. Hospitals, with their complex scheduling and inventory issues, can be managed more efficiently due to constant streams of data shared by the actual system and its twin. Experts say that implementing digital twin technology will create good jobs for tech workers. Those who understand how to maximize the benefits of digital twins are certain to be in high demand. Current staff at factories and hospitals that adopt digital twin technology can also thrive by upgrading their AI knowledge.

AI-Based Assistance for Elder Care

Another promising health care–related application for AI is in elder care. For seniors who spend too much time by themselves,

AI-powered robots and virtual companions can offer relief from loneliness. ElliQ from Intuition Robotics is marketed as an AI sidekick that helps provide safety and entertainment. The tabletop robot encourages seniors to be more active, connecting them with exercise videos, live bingo sessions, and video chats with loved ones. ElliQ also helps track an older person's vital signs and sends reminders about medications and doctor's appointments. It can carry on conversations that are spontaneous and contain details from prior chats. "[ElliQ] checks up on me. She finds out how I'm doing," says eighty-one-year-old Deanna Dezern. "She remembers little things like I wasn't happy yesterday."[39] Once plugged in for the first time, ElliQ even teaches its companions how to use it. Intuition Robotics can connect ElliQ to smart home features too, like smart thermostats, automatic lighting, and voice-activated appliances.

AI continues to make huge strides in personalizing devices that monitor a senior's health. Wearable devices can prevent medical disasters by tracking heart rates, detecting falls, and alerting caregivers in an emergency. A device such as CarePredict's AI-based monitor uses data to learn the patterns of its wearer's daily life. When something diverges from these patterns, the device alerts a caregiver or loved one. Some AI devices can even detect signs of early risk for Alzheimer's disease and other cognitive problems.

Despite the technical breakthroughs of AI, it cannot replace health care workers and their expertise. Their human skills of decision-making and empathy are essential to elder care. Mainly, AI tools will help health care workers do their job more quickly and efficiently.

Teaching Chatbots to Speak and Think

AI trainers have their own essential function. They teach generative AI to do its job more efficiently. Due to their fundamental role in GenAI, AI trainers seem assured of job security for the foreseeable future. They basically teach chatbots to speak, think, and interact with humans. They provide chatbots with lots of information, but

AI tools can help health care workers do their jobs more efficiently. Patients can video chat with their doctor while AI-powered tools gather and analyze information that the doctor can use later.

they choose information that is most useful for the chatbots' tasks. AI trainers facilitate communication between chatbots and people, trying to ensure that each understands the other. AI trainers strive to make a chatbot talk like a real person, one who is polite, helpful, friendly, and careful about questions of privacy. In other words, AI trainers provide chatbots with education and guidance. They are proof that chatbots are not out to steal someone's job. In fact, they cannot even function without assistance.

In the burgeoning world of GenAI, AI trainers tend to do many things at once. A conversation designer shapes how a chatbot talks to people. The goal is for its conversation to unfold naturally, like talking to a trusted friend. A model improver tries to make the chatbot perform complicated tasks more effectively. The key to accomplishing this is to make sure the chatbot understands what someone is saying to it. And that requires nuanced understanding—getting the subtle meaning of what is being said. A well-trained chatbot can often recognize the user's intent from the original prompt, without asking more questions. A data expert or data curator selects and prepares various data sets for the chatbot to access, while a technician connects the chatbot to other computer systems and troubleshoots errors or glitches. A technician also might choose appropriate machine-learning algorithms for the desired task. Some AI trainers also work with computer code, but it is not essential for the job.

Being a successful AI trainer calls for good language skills. Trainers must be able to explain things in simple language and understand what coworkers are saying. Much of the work is done alone, but the ability to coordinate with a team also comes in handy. Curiosity is useful, since AI trainers work in different areas, such as finance or health care, depending on the chatbot's focus. According to LinkedIn, AI trainers make from $50,000 to $115,000 a year. As generative AI proceeds in its global rollout, salaries for AI trainers are likely to rise.

In-House Positions Dealing with AI

In the future more companies are likely to hire AI instructors to teach their employees how to use AI. Instructors could present the basics of the technology or concentrate on teaching about the company's own in-house AI platform. Each time the company adopts a new AI tool or tweaks its database in some important way, the AI instructor could hold training sessions, conduct product demos, and be available for one-on-one sessions with employees. Some experts recommend instruction that is aimed at specific tasks and goals. "You need to have outcome-based training," says Kathleen Featheringham, director of artificial intelligence strategy at Booz Allen. "Focus on how AI can be used to push forward the mission of the organization, not just training for the sake of learning about AI."[40]

Companies that adopt GenAI solutions also need a bias analyst to check for biased or discriminatory material. The analyst could also review AI data sets to weed out data that inadvertently contains racist, sexist, or otherwise discriminatory language. For firms that use an AI-based hiring process, the bias analyst could review the system's algorithms for signs of unequal treatment. A hardworking bias analyst could save a company large sums by avoiding lawsuits and problems with government regulators.

The Importance of People Skills in Working with AI

For all the hand-wringing about job losses due to AI, employment experts say job markets in the future will still value so-called people skills. Surveys at LinkedIn show that 92 percent of executives in the United States consider people skills to be more important than ever. While AI doubtless will drive many changes in the workplace, workers who rely on skills such as sound judgment, problem solving, empathy, and active listening will always find themselves in demand. This goes along with the emerging

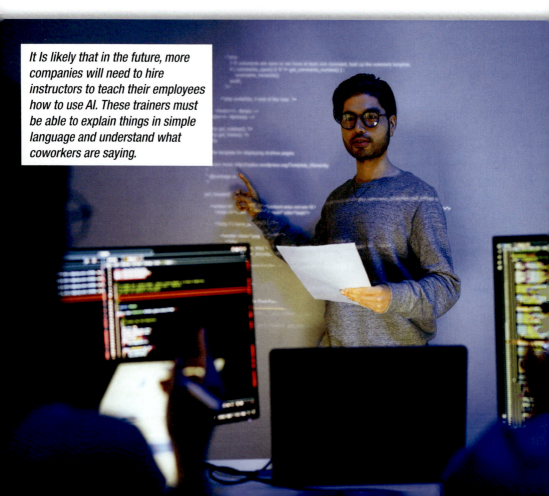

It Is likely that in the future, more companies will need to hire instructors to teach their employees how to use AI. These trainers must be able to explain things in simple language and understand what coworkers are saying.

consensus that AI will operate mainly as an assistant in the workplace and not the boss. After all, AI depends on detailed training and guidance to accomplish its basic tasks. Guiding the output of chatbots with practical supervision will assure the job security of office workers and technicians alike. As Nada Sanders and John Wood note in their recent study of boardroom opinions in *Harvard Business Review*, "While technical skills get more press, it is these uniquely human skills that companies need—and find to be in short supply in today's marketplace."[41]

> "While technical skills get more press, it is these uniquely human skills that companies need—and find to be in short supply in today's marketplace."[41]
>
> —Nada Sanders, professor of supply chain management at Northeastern University, and John Wood, attorney and educator

SOURCE NOTES

Introduction: An Explosion of New Jobs in AI

1. Quoted in Nik Popli, "The AI Job That Pays up to $335K—and You Don't Need a Computer Engineering Background," *Time*, April 14, 2023. www.time.com.
2. Quoted in Tim Bajarin, "The AI Generation: How Gen Z Will Shape the Future," *Forbes*, March 5, 2024. www.forbes.com.
3. Quoted in Randstad, "More than Half of Workers Believe AI Skills Will Future-Proof Their Careers, but Only 13% Have Been Offered Such Training Opportunities—Randstad Data Reveals," September 5, 2023. www.randstad.com.

Chapter One: How AI Is Reshaping the Workplace and the World

4. Quoted in Jack Kelly, "Indeed's New AI Tool Enhances Job Matches Between Employers and Candidates," *Forbes*, April 11, 2024. www.forbes.com.
5. imKranely, "Using AI for Brainstorming," Reddit, February 18, 2023. www.reddit.com.
6. Bernard Marr, "Generative AI Can Write Computer Code. Will We Still Need Software Developers?," *Forbes*, June 7, 2024. www.forbes.com.
7. Quoted in Andis Robeznieks, "AI Scribe Saves Doctors an Hour at the Keyboard Every Day," AMA, March 18, 2024. www.ama-assn.org.
8. Tom Shepherd and Stephanie Lomax, "Generative AI in the Legal Industry: The 3 Waves Set to Change How the Business Works," Thomson Reuters, February 27, 2024. www.thomsonreuters.com.
9. Maaz Khan, "Can Artificial Intelligence Replace Supply Chain Manager?," LinkedIn, March 29, 2023. www.linkedin.com.
10. Peter Brown et al., "How Young Workers Can Thrive with AI When They Have the Right Skills," World Economic Forum, July 15, 2024. www.weformum.org.

Chapter Two: Jobs and Careers in AI

11. Quoted in Jack Kelly, "'I Hope Suffering Happens to You': Nvidia CEO's Case for Hiring for Grit over Pedigree," *Forbes*, April 1, 2024. www.forbes.com.
12. Isabelle Bousquette, "Why Nvidia Is Now Tech's Hottest Employer," *Wall Street Journal* (podcast), February 29, 2024. www.wsj.com.

13. John Kim, "Nvidia's $2 Trillion Recruiting Playbook," Paraform, April 3, 2024. www.paraform.com.
14. Anne Nies, "The Ideal Machine Learning Engineer Candidate," LinkedIn, April 6, 2022. www.linkedin.com.
15. Quoted in Yolanda D. McGill, "Compliance Is Great but It Takes More to Excel in Fairness," Zest AI, August 5, 2024. www.zest.ai.
16. Quoted in Nick Fortuna, "AI vs. Financial Analysts: Who Is Better at Predicting Earnings of Public Firms?," *Wall Street Journal*, August 2, 2024. www.wsj.com.
17. Quoted in Brian Merchant, "AI Is Already Taking Jobs in the Video Game Industry," *Wired*, July 23, 2024. www.wired.com.
18. Quoted in Melissa Heikkila, "A Disney Director Tried—and Failed—to Use an AI Hans Zimmer to Create a Soundtrack," *MIT Technology Review*, September 19, 2023. www.technologyreview.com.

Chapter Three: Preparing for a Career in AI

19. Quoted in Katherine Bindley, "Tech Workers Retool for Artificial-Intelligence Boom," *Wall Street Journal*, May 26, 2024. www.wsj.com.
20. Quoted in Katherine Bindley, "The Fight for AI Talent: Pay Million-Dollar Packages and Buy Whole Teams," *Wall Street Journal*, March 27, 2024. www.wsj.com.
21. Quoted in Bindley, "Tech Workers Retool for Artificial-Intelligence Boom."
22. Michael B. Horn, "Artificial Intelligence, Real Anxiety," *Education Next*, January 31, 2024. www.educationnext.org.
23. Quoted in Cheryl Winokur Munk, "Colleges Are Touting AI Degree Programs. Here's How to Decide If It's Worth the Cost," CNBC, March 2, 2024. www.cnbc.com.
24. Michael Stedman, "4 Steps to Start Your Career in Artificial Intelligence," Yoh, March 20, 2024. www.yoh.com.
25. Quoted in Dave Zielinski, "Employers Train Employees to Close the AI Skills Gap," SHRM, March 8, 2024. www.shrm.org.
26. Bart Ziegler, "The Best Ways to Ask ChatGPT Questions," *Wall Street Journal*, May 12, 2024. www.wsj.com.
27. Quoted in Ziegler, "The Best Ways to Ask ChatGPT Questions."

Chapter Four: Challenges of Working with AI

28. Quoted in Martin Coulter and Greg Bensinger, "Alphabet Shares Dive After Google AI Chatbot Bard Flubs Answer in Ad," Reuters, February 8, 2023. www.reuters.com.

29. Quoted in James Vincent, "Google's AI Chatbot Bard Makes Factual Error in First Demo," The Verge, February 8, 2023. www.theverge.com.
30. Harry Guinness, "What Are AI Hallucinations and How Do You Prevent Them?," Zapier, July 10, 2024. www.zapier.com.
31. Lionel Bascles, "All In on AI, Understanding AI Bias & Fairness," Sanofi, July 3, 2024. www.sanofi.com.
32. Quoted in Mike Thomas, "14 Risks and Dangers of Artificial Intelligence (AI)," Built In, July 25, 2024. https://builtin.com.
33. Kate Crawford and Jason Schultz, "Generative AI Is a Crisis for Copyright Law," *Issues in Science and Technology,* January 16, 2024. https://issues.org.

Chapter Five: A Bright Future for a New Technology

34. Quoted in McKinsey & Company, "Mars Exploration Pushes the Boundaries of AI: An Interview with NASA's Vandi Verma," January 9, 2023. www.mckinsey.com.
35. Quoted in McKinsey & Company, "Mars Exploration Pushes the Boundaries of AI."
36. Quoted in Eric Betz, "The Skycrane: How NASA's Perseverance Rover Will Land on Mars," *Astronomy,* February 18, 2021. www.astronomy.com.
37. Quoted in NASA, "Twin of NASA's Perseverance Mars Rover Begins Terrain Tests," NASA, November 17, 2021, www.nasa.gov.
38. Quoted in Sai Balasubramainian, "Digital Twin Technology Has the Potential to Radically Disrupt Healthcare," *Forbes,* December 22, 2023. www.forbes.com.
39. Quoted in "User Stories," ElliQ, 2024. https://elliq.com.
40. Quoted in Tom Taulli, "Artificial Intelligence: Should You Teach It to Your Employees?," *Forbes,* September 10, 2021. www.forbes.com.
41. Quoted in Joe McKendrick, "AI Skills or AI-Enhanced Skills? What Employers Need Could Depend on You," ZDNet, June 17, 2024. www.zdnet.com.

INTERVIEW WITH A SOFTWARE DEVELOPER

Mark Hoffman is a senior software engineer and software developer with more than thirty years of experience in backend services such as database management and security service. He has worked as a staff developer at PayPal, State Street Bank, and several start-up firms. He is currently providing AI solutions as an independent software developer. He works remotely from his home in St. Petersburg, Florida, or as a "digital nomad" from various tropical locales.

Q: How did you become proficient in using AI?
A: I started to learn AI by reading a ChatGPT tutorial and watching a number of YouTube videos on the subject. After that, I experimented with a small demo program to get a better understanding of AI's capabilities. I also read articles about the underlying technology, such as explanations of large language models (LLMs). I have continued to refine how I write my prompts for GenAI to maximize my productivity.

Q: Can you describe how you use AI during your typical workday?
A: I do not use AI every day, but I employ it quite frequently for certain tasks. For example, it is most useful when I'm starting a project or writing documentation for a project. For example, I use AI to better understand a problem that I'm working on or as an aid to write a function or set of functions for a development process that I'm unfamiliar with.

Q: What are the advantages of using AI in your work?
A: Using AI can greatly increase my productivity by significantly reducing the amount of boilerplate computer code that I have to write. Boilerplate code is the name for sections of code that are standard and repetitive and must appear in certain places in

a software project. It provides a foundation and structure for the task you're working on. Writing repetitive code from scratch can waste a lot of time. But by writing a correct prompt for boilerplate code, I can save myself several steps in the coding process.

Also, AI is very helpful in saving time when I am learning a new technology. I can ask it very targeted questions and receive exactly the information I need, instead of going through a tutorial or watching a video in hopes that the subject matter that I'm interested in is included. ChatGPT is also great for generating documentation that I can curate and wordsmith. Documentation is material that allows users to use a product more completely in order to meet their specific needs. It's often a combination of technical information and user tips that may not be obvious from the software itself and need to be explained. AI's assistance with documentation can get me up and running very quickly.

Q: What drawbacks or problems have you encountered in using AI?
A: Actually the biggest drawback is relying too heavily on AI. It's important to remember that it can make mistakes both small and large, and it can even fabricate information at times—with glitches called hallucinations.

In my work, it is necessary to write unit tests against AI-generated code. Unit tests are a set of tests done at the coding level to verify that individual software units, such as functions or methods, are functioning correctly. AI can check itself by reading and analyzing its own generated code. It can even detect plagiarism in code that has been modified in some way. At any rate, unit tests help you get a much better understanding of what code was generated by AI. You need to apply the old adage: Trust but verify!

Q: What personal qualities do you find most valuable in your work with AI?
A: Probably the two best personal qualities to possess when working with AI are patience and thoroughness. You want to

be very thorough in vetting the AI-generated output, whether it is boilerplate or some new combination. If you are using AI to generate code, you have to examine the code and test it just as if a human had produced it. This requires tremendous patience and attention to detail. You never want to become complacent and rubberstamp AI-generated code or documentation. This can have disastrous effects on a project.

Q: What advice do you have for students who might be interested in an AI-related job or career?
A: My main advice is just to experiment with AI and get to understand its strengths and weaknesses. Watch videos, read articles, and also make an effort to understand how LLMs work to gain a solid foundation with the technology. As mentioned before, you mustn't be complacent or lazy in expecting that AI will always produce the desired output or correct answer.

AI users must also stay up to date with changes in the industry by reading blogs and frequently news sites that cover the AI industry. This is especially important if you plan to specialize, like myself, in using AI to assist your software development efforts.

FIND OUT MORE

Books

Steve Ballenger, *Future of Work: AI, Automation, and Employment.* Oldham, UK: Digital Phoenix Media, 2024.

Kavita Ganesan, *The Business Case for AI: A Leader's Guide to AI Strategies, Best Practices & Real-World Applications.* Salt Lake City, UT: Opinosis Analytics, 2022.

Russel Grant, *Prompt Engineering and ChatGPT: How to Easily 10X Your Productivity, Creativity, and Make More Money Without Working Harder.* Pebblefalls Publishing, 2023.

Kai-Fu Lee and Chen Qiufan, *AI 2041: Ten Visions for Our Future.* New York: Crown Currency, 2021.

Ethan Mollick, *Co-Intelligence: Living and Working with AI.* New York: Portfolio, 2024.

Internet Sources

Theresa Agovino, "The Promise and Peril of Artificial Intelligence," SHRM, May 12, 2023. www.shrm.org.

Nacho De Marco, "AI Isn't Here to Replace Jobs—It's Freeing People to Be People Again," *Forbes*, May 12, 2023. www.forbes.com.

Ashton Jackson, "3 Ways to Use AI Right Now to Get Ahead—If You Do, You're 'Really Going to Succeed,' Says Expert," CNBC, September 25, 2023. www.cnbc.com.

Ryan Roslansky, "The AI-Fueled Future of Work Needs Humans More than Ever," *Wired*, January 28, 2024. www.wired.com.

Mike Thomas, "The Future of AI: How Artificial Intelligence Will Change the World," Built In, March 13, 2024. https://builtin.com.

Marc Zao-Sanders, "How People Are Really Using GenAI," *Harvard Business Review*, March 19, 2024. https://hbr.org.

Organizations and Websites

AI Job Board
https://theaijobboard.com
The AI Job Board promotes its website as the number one listing on the internet for jobs in artificial intelligence and machine learning. It finds

hundreds of companies hiring in the AI space around the world. Its listings include job descriptions and requirements for AI jobs, including remote and entry-level positions.

Brookings Institution
www.brookings.edu
The Brookings Institution is a nonprofit organization devoted to in-depth research to improve policy and governance at local, national, and global levels. Issues about AI make up an important part of its website content. A recent article titled "Will Apple's Foray into the AI Space Be 'for the Rest of Us'?" looks at issues of human bias and data security risks in Apple's new AI rollout.

Hoover Institution
www.hoover.org
The Hoover Institution is an American public policy think tank that promotes economic liberty and prosperity, free enterprise, and limited government. Its website includes several articles that look at AI's rapid rise and life-changing possibilities, as well as its possible drawbacks.

Liquid Web
www.liquidweb.com
This tech blog features excellent material explaining AI in clear language. In "Artificial Intelligence (AI) for Beginners—What Is AI?," blogger Luke Cavanagh looks at the technology, dispels common misconceptions, and provides definitions of key terms. The site's bloggers provide accessible information on AI that is helpful to beginners as well as more experienced users.

MIT Technology Review
www.technologyreview.com
The magazine *MIT Technology Review* discusses the latest news and issues from the world of high tech. Its material on AI deals with ways that this technology is affecting various industries and the modern workplace. Two recent articles on its website are "Here's How People Are Actually Using AI" and "We Finally Have a Definition for Open-Source AI."

Virginia Tech Engineer
https://eng.vt.edu/magazine
The web magazine *Virginia Tech Engineer* presents expert articles on cutting edge technologies and related issues. The Fall 2023 edition, titled "AI—the Good, the Bad, and the Scary," includes analyses of AI by the faculty of Virginia Tech's College of Engineering. Faculty experts range from computer scientists to electrical engineers to aerospace engineers.

INDEX

Note: Boldface page numbers indicate illustrations

AI boot camps, 8, 31–33
AI educator/trainer, 7, 49–51
AI Job Board (website), 60–61
AI Overviews (AI-based search engine), 37
Ajder, Henry, 26
Alexa (virtual assistant), 10
Alzheimer's disease, AI in prediction of, 48
art/entertainment, 24–26
　copyright issues with, 42–44
artificial intelligence (AI)/AI apps
　in art/entertainment, 24–26
　in banking/finance, 22–24
　biased results in, 39–40
　in health care, 13–15
　infrastructure, job opportunities in, 22
　in law offices, 15
　skills in, importance in job marketplace, 21–22
　in warehouse/supply chain management, 15–17, **16**
　workplace tasks performed by, 6–7, 10–12

banking/finance, 22–24
Bard (chatbot), 36–37, **38**
Bascles, Lionel, 40
Bernstein, Anna, 5
bias analyst, 51
bias/discrimination
　in AI results, 39–40
Blair, Tony, 41
Booth School of Business (University of Chicago), 23–24
Bousquette, Isabelle, 19
Brookings Institution, 61

careers, AI
　general information about, **4**
　planning for, 7–8
chatbots, 10
　AI trainers and, 49–51
　writing prompts for, 33–34
ChatGPT (generative AI platform), 11, 18, 38
　code writing with, 12
　importance of human operator in, 24
　salaries for workers in, 28
　use by teachers vs. students, 30
　writing prompts for, 33–34
Chung, Caroline, 48
college, AI programs in, 30–31
compliance expert, 24
computed tomography (CT), 14
conversation designer, 50
Copilot (GenAI platform), 12, 28, 34
copyright
　AI-created works not eligible for, 43–44
　infringements of, 42–43
Coursera (online course provider), 32
Crawford, Kate, 44

data scientist, 7
deepfakes, 40–42, **41**
DeviantArt (AI art program), 42
Dezern, Deanna, 49
Dhanani, Asif, 27, 33
digital twins technology, 46–48

education/training requirements, **4**, 7–8
Edwards, Gareth, 26
edX (online course provider), 32
elder care, AI-based assistance for, 48–49
ElliQ (AI-powered elder care robot), 49
entertainment. *See* art/entertainment
ethics officer, 7

Fair Diffusion (AI tool), 42
Featheringham, Kathleen, 51
finance. *See* banking/finance
Flynn, Maria, 30–31
Ford, Martin, 41–42
Francis (pope), 41

generative AI (GenAI) platforms, 11
   potential for errors/hallucinations in, 37
   in writing computer code, 12–13
   writing prompts for, 33–34
Generative AI in Practice (Marr), 12
Google Nest (doorbell app), 10
Govindarajan, Jayesh, 28
Guinness, Harry, 39
Guterres, António, 41

hallucinations, 28, 36–37, 44, 58
   steps to avoid, 38–39
Harvard Business Review (journal), 53
health care, 13–15
   bias in AI and, 39
   digital twins technology in, 48
high school curricula, AI related, 28–30
Hoffman, Mark, 57–59
Hoover Institution, 61
Horn, Allison, 33
Horn, Michael B., 30

Huang, Jensen, 18–19

inventory management, 15–17, **16**

JAMA Network Open (journal), 14

Kamkar, Sean, 23
Khan, Maaz, 16–17
Kim, John, 20

law offices, 15
Lee, Kristine, 13
LexisNexis (data analytics firm), 15
LinkedIn (job search website), 21, 51, 52
Liquid Web (blog), 61
Lomax, Stephanie, 15

machine-learning (ML) engineer, 7, 21–22
Marr, Bernard, 12, 13
Mars rover, 45–46, **47**
Martin, Bryan, 46–47
Midjourney (AI art app), 24–25, 40, 42, **43**
MIT Technology Review (magazine, website), 61
Mukherjee, Raj, 9
music platforms, generative, 25–26

Nature Medicine (journal), 14
Nies, Anne, 22
Nikolaev, Valeri V., 24
Nvidia (computer chip manufacturer), 18, 19–20, 26

online AI courses/boot camps, 8, 31–33
opinion polls. *See* surveys
OPTIMISM (Mars rover replica), 46–47

people skills, importance in AI work, 52–53
Permanente Medical Group, 13
Perseverance (*Percy*, Mars rover), 45–46, **47**
polls. *See* surveys
privacy violations, 44
problems in AI
  bias/discrimination, 38–40
  copyright issues, 42–44
  deepfakes/deliberate deception, 40–42, **41**
  errors/hallucinations, 36–37
  privacy issues, 44
prompt engineer/engineering, 5
  practice in, 33–34
prompts, AI
  tips for writing, 31

Rao, Naveen, 28
robotic process automation (RPA), 17

salaries, **4**
  of AI trainers, 51
  of GenAI workers, 28
Sanders, Nada, 53
Schultz, Jason, 44
Shepherd, Tom, 15
Siri (virtual assistant), 10
Skycrane (simulated Mars landing maneuver), 46
SmartSourcing (AI-based tool), 9, **11**
software developer
  interview with, 57–59
Stability AI (art program), 42–43
Stable Diffusion (AI art app), 24–25
Stedman, Michael, 31–32
STEM (science, technology, engineering, mathematics) classes, 28–29

Surace, Kevin, 5
surveys
  of CEOs on AI impacts on business landscape, 7
  of executives on importance of people skills, 30
  on importance of AI skills in hiring, 21
  of lawyers on AI in legal research, 15
  on on-the-job AI training, 33
  on use of AI by teachers *vs.* students, 30

Tang, Alice, 48
Technical University of Darmstadt, 42
Tremblay, Grant, 36–37

Udacity (online course provider), 32
University of California, San Francisco (UCSF), 48

van 't Noordende, Sander, 8
Verma, Vandi, 45–46
Virginia Tech Engineer (website), 61
virtual assistant, 10

Walton Family Foundation, 30
warehouse management, 15–17, **16**
West, Martin, 30
Wood, John, 53
World Economic Forum, 17

Zest FairBoost (credit-check software), 23
Ziegler, Bart, 34
Zimmer, Hans, 26